THE
CHANGING
WORLD OF
RETIREMENT
PLANNING

Place label here. Include:

Instructor name(s)

FINRA member firm

Broker-dealer disclosure

THE CHANGING WORLD OF RETIREMENT PLANNING

Copyright © 2018, The National Society of Financial Educators™

All rights reserved.

Printed in the United States of America

ISBN: 978-1-981513-11-6

All rights reserved. No part of this book may be reproduced or transmitted in any form or by any means, electronic or mechanical, including photocopying, recording, or by any information storage and retrieval system, without written permission of the author, except for the inclusion of brief quotations in a review.

This publication is designed to provide accurate and authoritative information with regard to the subject matter covered. It is sold with the understanding that the publisher is not engaged in rendering legal, accounting, or other professional advice. If legal advice or other expert assistance is required, the services of a competent professional should be sought.

The information in this book is for general use and, while we believe the information is reliable and accurate, it is important to remember individual situations may be entirely different. Therefore, information should be relied upon only when coordinated with individual professional tax and/or financial advice. You need to consider your specific situation including your health and legacy goals before acting on any information presented in this book. Please note that neither the information presented nor any opinion expressed is to be considered as an offer to buy or purchase any insurance or securities products and services referenced in this book.

The information provided is not intended as tax or legal advice and may not be relied on for the purpose of avoiding any individual Federal or State tax penalties. The National Society of Financial Educators, your instructor, their employees or representatives are not authorized to give tax or legal advice. Individuals are encouraged to seek advice from their own tax and legal counsel. They are also encouraged to seek advice from their own financial and/or insurance professional.

Typesetting by *Wordzworth.com*

Contents

Retiring in the 21st Century

Introduction	1-1
The Old Paradigm	1-2
The New Paradigm	1-3
Summary	1-4

Tax Rate Risk

Introduction	2-1
The Old Paradigm	2-2
The New Paradigm	2-3
Where Did My Deductions Go?	2-4
A Brief History of Tax Rates	2-5
Are Taxes Going Up or Down?	2-6
What Are Our Country's Biggest Expenses?	2-7
Will Taxes Go Up?	2-8
Historical Precedence	2-9
Could Tax Rates Really Double?	2-10
U.S. Debt vs. Interest on Debt	2-11
In Summary	2-12

Retirement Distribution Planning

Introduction	3-1
The Old Paradigm	3-2
The New Paradigm	3-3

What is Retirement Distribution Planning?	3-4
The Taxable Bucket	3-5
The Double Compounding Problem	3-6
Comparison: Taxable vs. Tax-Advantaged	3-7
The Tax-Deferred Bucket	3-8
Required Minimum Distributions	3-9
Benefits of Tax-Deferred Investing	3-10
The Tax-Advantaged Bucket	3-11
Tax-Deferred or Tax-Advantaged?	3-12
In Summary	3-13

Maximizing Social Security

Introduction	4-1
What is Provisional Income?	4-2
Example of Social Security Taxation	4-3
Social Security Taxation	4-4
Avoiding Social Security Taxation	4-5
Pensions and Social Security Taxation	4-6
In Summary	4-7

Long-Term Care Planning

Introduction	5-1
The Old Paradigm	5-2
The New Paradigm	5-3
Medicaid Spend-down Rules	5-4
How Will You Pay for Long-Term Care Expenses?	5-5
In Summary	5-6

SECTION ONE

Retiring in the 21ˢᵗ Century

Introduction

Everyone wants something different from retirement. No one person's retirement is going to look exactly like another's. Your greatest challenge may be to identify what *you* want most out of this new chapter of your life.

In this workshop, we will:

1. Review "traditional" retirement paradigms
2. Identify new paradigms and discuss how they affect you
3. Help you build a plan to get the most out of your retirement

The Changing World of Retirement Planning — Section 1–1

The Old Paradigm

Approaching retirement like your parents approached it may not yield the best results. By contrasting the old retirement paradigm with the new retirement paradigm, you may be better prepared to get the most out of your retirement years.

Your parents' retirement may have consisted of the following:

- Work for the same company their whole career
- Retire at 65 and receive a pension
- Pension covered most lifestyle expenses
- Rely upon Social Security only for supplemental income
- Put less emphasis on one's own investments

The Changing World of Retirement Planning   Section 1–2

The New Paradigm

Your parents wouldn't recognize the world of retirement planning into which most retirees are now venturing. How do you chart a course in this changing world of retirement planning? Retirees these days need a plan more than ever. Your retirement will likely be much different than that of your parents.

The following are a few reasons why:

- Average person now works for 7 different companies during career
- The 401(k) replaced the pension for many
- Retirement for many is mostly self-funded
- Social Security may cover very little of lifestyle requirements
- Some never fully retire but choose to stay engaged at some level.

Summary

- It's as important to know what you're retiring to as it is what you're retiring from
- Your retirement will likely look much different than the generation that came before you
- You will have to adopt updated paradigms as you plan your retirement

Throughout this course we will identify some of the new "paradigms" facing a new generation of retirees. Navigating these new paradigms will be critical to the success of your retirement in the 21st century.

SECTION TWO
Tax Rate Risk

Introduction

Many Americans have saved the lion's share of their retirement in tax-deferred accounts like 401(k)s and IRAs because of the perceived tax advantages. Today, however, we are marching into a future where our nation's debt load is at an all-time high and threatening to spiral out of control. What does this hold for the future of tax rates in America? If tax rates go up, how will this impact your cash flow in retirement?

In this section we will discuss the following:

- Why tax rates could double
- How our nation's debt may force tax rates to rise over time
- The extent to which our nation's entitlement programs are underfunded
- How rising tax rates may affect your cash flow in retirement
- How lost deductions may affect your tax burden in retirement

The Changing World of Retirement Planning — Section 2-1

The Old Paradigm

The "old" tax paradigm as it relates to retirement planning states that:

- You will be living on less income in retirement
- You will therefore be in a lower tax bracket
- Given this lower tax bracket, tax-deferred investing is the best

Mathematically speaking, if you're going to be in a lower tax bracket in retirement, it makes sense to invest the vast majority of your retirement dollars in tax-deferred accounts like 401(k)s and IRAs. But will you *really* be in a lower tax bracket in retirement?

The New Paradigm

The "new" tax paradigm says that, in all actuality, your tax bracket in retirement may be higher than it is today.

This may be for a number of different reasons:

- You may need just as much income in retirement as you did during your working years
- Your marginal tax bracket may rise due to our country's fiscal challenges
- You may lose many of your greatest tax deductions in retirement

Where Did My Deductions Go?

Many of the deductions you experienced during your working years vanish right when you need them the very most: at retirement. The following are some of the larger deductions you may lose by the time you reach retirement:

- Interest on your mortgage
- Qualified retirement plan contributions (401k, 403b, etc.)
- Children – Tax Credit
- Charity – many retirees donate time, not money

Many of these deductions during your working years may have added up to anywhere from $40,000 to $70,000.

Typical Deductions in Retirement

Absent these traditional deductions in retirement, most retirees are left with the following:

- Standard Deduction ($24,000)

Because of this loss of deductions, it is possible to be in a higher tax bracket in retirement while living on less income.

A Brief History of Tax Rates

It's important to understand the history of tax rates so that we recognize that tax rates today are likely as low as we'll experience in our lifetime. Given our country's fiscal challenges, how much longer can we enjoy historically low tax rates?

Top marginal tax rates

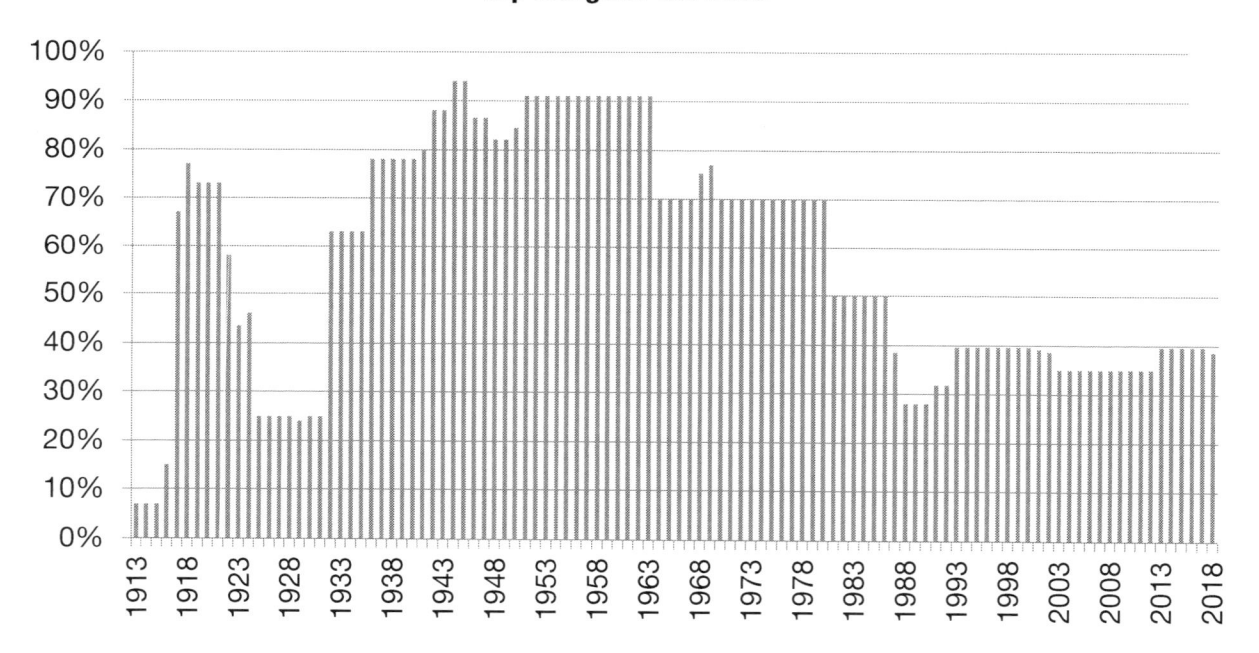

Source: www.taxpolicycenter.org/statistics/historical-highest-marginal-income-tax-rates

Highlights:

- The last two years of World War II, the highest marginal tax bracket was 94%
- Throughout the entire decade of the 70s, taxes hovered around 70%
- In 2018, the highest tax bracket is 37%, near historical lows

Are Taxes Going Up or Down?

As we move forward in time, to 2026, 2030 and beyond, will tax rates be higher or lower than they are today? The following are a few factors that (absent a dramatic reduction in spending) could force tax rates to rise:

- Social Security
- Medicare and Medicaid
- Interest on the National Debt
- Fannie Mae and Freddie Mac
- Department of Defense
- The Prescription Drug Program for Seniors
- Pension Obligations
- Etc.

Many of these are what the government calls "unfunded liabilities". An unfunded liability is a promise the government has made that it has no way of honoring. Some calculations put these total unfunded obligations at close to $120 trillion![1]

---

[1] nypost.com/2011/06/26/120-trillion-the-shocking-true-size-of-our-nations-debt/

What Are Our Country's Biggest Expenses?

Which of the aforementioned "unfunded liabilities" will, if not addressed, be the greatest contributors to our nation's increased debt load?

- Social Security
- Medicare and Medicaid

As of 2017, 71% of every tax dollar that comes into the US Treasury goes to pay for only four things:

- Social Security
- Medicare
- Medicaid
- Interest on our national debt

As Baby Boomers leave the work force and move onto the roles of entitlement programs, this landscape will begin to change. By 2020, those 4 expenses will consume 92% of all tax revenue flowing into the US Treasury.[2] This leaves 8 cents of every tax dollar to pay for everything else! Let's take a look at what "everything else" entails:

---

[2] www.federal-budjet.insidegov.com/1/120/2017-Estimate, http://money.cnn.com/2011/01/21/news/economy/spending_taxes_debt/index.htm.

Children's nutrition, Border Security, Food Safety and Inspection Service, disaster relief, U.S. Forest Service, Drug Enforcement Administration, Public Housing Program, IRS, Animal and Plant Health Inspection, federal courts, Bureau of Indian Affairs, NASA, Army, National Endorsement for the Arts, Air Force, federal student loans, Rural Development, Coast Guard, Food Stamps, National Park Service, income assistance, Department of Family Services, research and development, U.S. Geological Survey, Environmental Protection Agency, Centers for Disease Control and Prevention, FEMA, Immigration and Customs Enforcement, Secret Service, FAA, Supportive Housing for the Elderly Program, Federal Railroad Administration, Navy, Bureau of Land Management, federal pension system, Peace Corps, FCC, State Department, National Science Foundation, Congress, Fish and Wildlife Service, White House, SEC, Smithsonian Institute, Small Business Administration, FBI, Federal Highway Administration...[3]

---

[3] http://money.cnn.com/2011/01/21/news/economy/spending_taxes_debt/index.htm.

Will Taxes Go Up?

David Walker

David Walker was the Comptroller General of the federal government from 1997 to 2008 under Presidents Bush and Clinton. He was the head of the Government Accountability Office (GAO), and served on the board of Social Security for 7 years. He may know more about our country's fiscal condition than anyone. He said this about the prospect of higher taxes:

> "Regardless of what politicians tell you, any additional accumulations of debt are, absent dramatic reductions in the size and role of government, basically deferred tax increases…Unless we begin to get our fiscal house in order, there's simply no other way to handle our ever-mounting debt burdens except by doubling taxes over time."[4]

---

[4] David Walker, "Commentary: Why Your Taxes Could Double", CNN.com, April 15, 2009, http://www.cnn.com/2009/POLITICS/04/15/walker.tax.debt/

Forbes Magazine

Here's what Forbes magazine had to say about taxing the rich as a means of solving our nation's fiscal crisis:

> *"The problem is that there are not enough 'high income earners' to satisfy today's debt and deficits. This means that middle income America will soon be in the scope of the Congressional rifle...Because the poor have nothing to tax, the middle class will be forced to ante up."*[5]

The Congressional Budget Office

Finally, in 2008, the Congressional Budget Office (CBO) was asked to project how high tax rates would have to go to pay for Social Security, Medicare, and Medicaid. This is what they said:

> *"If Social Security, Medicare and Medicaid go unchanged, the rate for the lowest bracket would increase from 10% to 25%; the tax rate on incomes in the current 25% bracket would have to be increased to 63%; and the tax rate of the highest bracket would have to be raised from 35% to 88%."*

---

[5] http://www.cbo.gov/ftpdocs/92xx/doc9216/05-19-LongtermBudget_Letter-to-Ryan.pdf

Historical Precedence

Before we explore the possibility of *higher* tax rates in the future, let's remind ourselves of how low tax rates are today. Our tax system in our country works in the following way. Some of your money is taxed at 10%, some at 12, some at 22, some at 24, some at 32, some at 35, and some at 37%.

| **2018** | 10% | 12% | 22% | 24% | 32% | 35% | 37% |

According to the CBO, absent any reduction in spending, these are the levels to which tax rates would have to rise to keep our country solvent:

| **Future** | 25% | 63% | 88% |

Many are skeptical when faced with the prospect of higher tax rates. You don't have to go very far back in the history of our country, however, to find tax rates that were that high. From 1960 to 1963, tax rates in our country were the following:

| **1960–63** | 26% | 38% | 56% | 69% | 78% | 87% |

There is historical precedence to suggest that tax rates in the future could rise, and in dramatic fashion.

Section 2–9 *The Changing World of Retirement Planning*

Could Tax Rates Really Double?

Tax Rates Around the World

We are one of the only industrialized nations in the world that doesn't have tax rates that approach the 50% mark.[6]

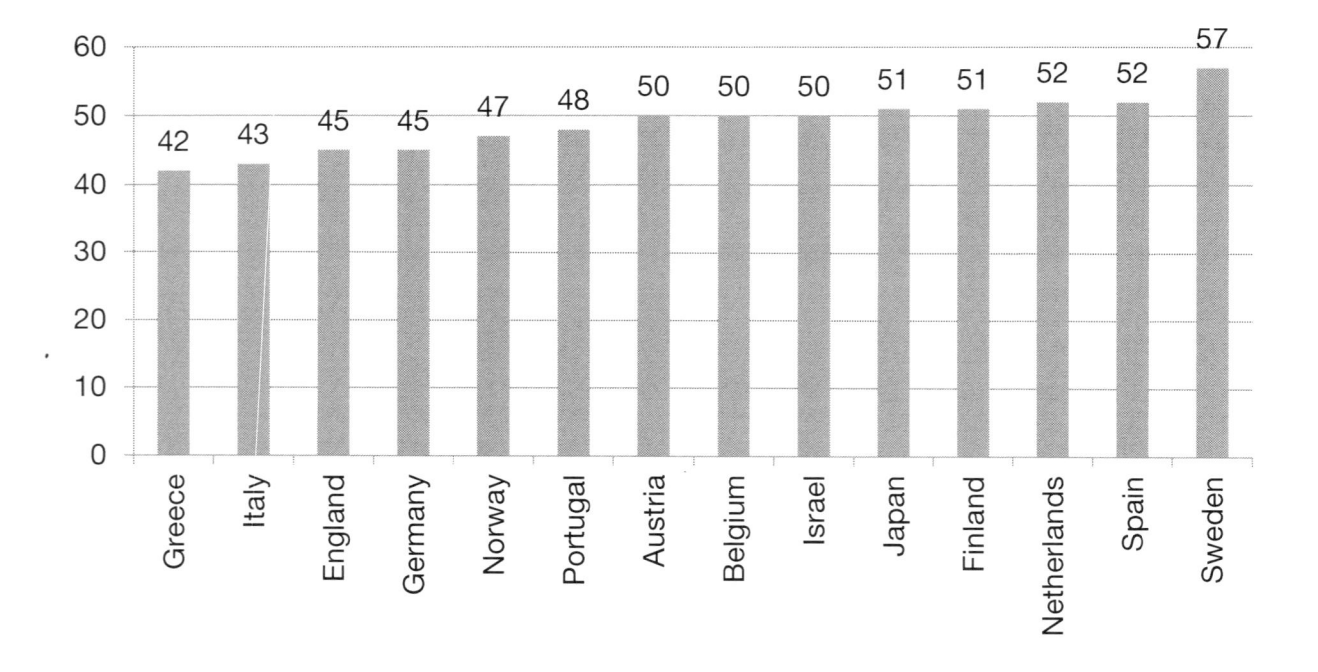

Country	Rate
Greece	42
Italy	43
England	45
Germany	45
Norway	47
Portugal	48
Austria	50
Belgium	50
Israel	50
Japan	51
Finland	51
Netherlands	52
Spain	52
Sweden	57

The math suggests that, absent any spending cuts, we may soon be joining the ranks of countries around the world whose tax rates are at or above 50%.

[6] http://www.kpmg.com/global/en/services/tax/tax-tools-and-resources/pages/individual-income-tax-rates-table.aspx

The Changing World of Retirement Planning Section 2-10

U.S. Debt vs. Interest on Debt

In the Year 2000

In the year 2000, our national debt was $5.6 Trillion, yet the cost of servicing that debt was an astounding $222 Billion.

In the Year 2018

Today, our national debt is $21 Trillion. Yet, when we look at the annual interest we're paying on that $21 Trillion, it's about $277 Billion. That's only $55 Billion more than what we were paying 17 years ago when the debt was less than a third as much as it is today.[7]

Why are the Costs of Debt Service in 2000 & 2018 so similar?

The reason debt service today is so similar to that of the year 2000 is due to one simple fact: interest rates today are at historically low levels. They have never been this low for this long. If interest rates were to return to historically normal levels, what would happen to the cost to service our national debt on an annual basis? It would more than triple!

For that reason, even if we somehow solved the underfunding problems associated with Social Security, Medicare and Medicaid, we could still have a major problem with our $21 Trillion dollar national debt. If interest rates rise to normal levels, our government may have no other choice but to raise taxes.

[7] Usdebtclock.org

In Summary

In this section we learned that:

- Absent dramatic and permanent spending cuts, tax rates in the future are likely to be much higher than they are today
- There is historical precedence for higher taxes
- You will not likely have as many deductions in retirement as you did during your working years
- Retirement accounts like 401(k)s and IRAs may be exposed to inordinate amounts of tax rate risk

SECTION THREE

Retirement Distribution Planning

Introduction

Accumulating dollars in the right types of accounts can be just as important as growing them in the right investments. In this section we will cover the following:

- The three basic types of retirement accounts
- How to contribute to these accounts in order to maximize cash flow in retirement
- What's better: tax-deferred, tax-advantaged or both?
- How to define a "true" tax-advantaged investment
- When you should convert your IRA to a Roth IRA
- How distributions from IRAs and 401(k)s affect Social Security taxation
- Strategies to reduce or eliminate taxes in retirement

Section 3-1

The Changing World of Retirement Planning

The Old Paradigm

The old retirement paradigm always worked under the premise that your taxes were going to be substantially lower in retirement than during your working years. In this case, it made sense to accumulate the lion's share of your assets in tax-deferred accounts. The thinking was, get a deduction at higher tax rates in order to postpone the payment of those taxes until much later in life when your tax rate was likely to be lower.

The New Paradigm

Your tax picture during your retirement may differ from that of your parents in the following ways:

- You may need as much income in your retirement years as you did during your working years
- Our country's fiscal challenges may force tax rates higher
- You may lose many of your greatest tax deductions in retirement
- You may be in a higher tax bracket in retirement than you were during your working years
- Accumulating dollars thoughtfully and proactively in a variety of retirement accounts may extend the life of your retirement assets

What is Retirement Distribution Planning?

Retirement Distribution Planning can be defined as the following:

"Accumulating the right amount of money in the right types of accounts in order to maximize cash flow in retirement."

The 3 Types of Investment Accounts

There are many different types of investments that you can utilize to save for retirement. However, all of those investments fit into only three basic types of accounts. During this course, we will refer to these accounts as buckets of money. They are as follows:

- The Taxable Bucket
- The Tax-Deferred Bucket
- The Tax-Advantaged Bucket

If tax rates in the future are likely to be higher than they are today, then we need to be very thoughtful and intentional about how we accumulate dollars in these types of accounts. Failing to do so may cause us to pay hundreds of thousands of dollars in avoidable taxes in retirement.

To better understand the importance of accumulating the right amounts of money in the right types of accounts, let's begin by identifying the pros and cons of each bucket.

The Taxable Bucket

In this bucket, you pay taxes if your money grows, regardless of whether you take money out. The following are a few examples of taxable investments:

- Savings Accounts
- Money Markets
- CDs
- Mutual Funds
- Stocks
- Bonds
- Etc.

The tipoff that you have taxable investments is the 1099 you receive from your financial institution at the end of each year. The 1099 reports to the IRS the amount of taxable income you received from a given investment. The taxable bucket has pros and cons which help you understand how to best incorporate it into your retirement savings plan.

Pros

- Generally Liquid (accessible)[8]

---

[8] The value of stocks, bonds and mutual funds can rise and fall with the market which may make them less liquid than other taxable alternatives

Cons

- Growth is taxable
- 1099s from these accounts may cause your Social Security to be taxed (more about this in Section 5)

Because taxable investments are generally liquid, the taxable bucket makes for a good emergency fund. It is generally recommended that you have 6 months' worth of living expenses in your emergency fund.[9]

Risks Associated with a Balance That Is Too Large

- Inflation risk (due to the low rates of return of some of the more traditional taxable accounts, i.e., CDs, money markets, savings, etc.)
- Tax inefficiency
- The Double Compounding Problem

---

[9] The value of stocks, bonds and mutual funds can rise and fall with the market which may make them less liquid than other taxable alternatives

The Double Compounding Problem

The Double Compounding Problem occurs when you grow your money in your taxable bucket while tax rates rise steadily over time.

Consider this example: Let's say that you make a contribution of $100,000 to a taxable investment which earns 5% per year. Because this investment is taxable, you would pay tax at your marginal tax rate, both federal and state (if applicable). In this example, we'll use 24% federal and 6% state tax for a total of 30%. By the end of the first year, your pre-tax investment return is $5,000. But when we figure in taxes at the 30% rate, your true after-tax return is only $3,500.

In the following chart, we continue down this road for 10 years, raising taxes by 1% with each passing year. By the 10th year, you can see the true impact of this double compounding effect: a 74% increase in your tax bill!

Year	Combined Federal and State Tax Rate	Annual Balance	Pre-tax Investment Income at 5% Growth	After-tax Investment Income	Total Tax Bill
1	30%	$100,000	$5,000	$3,500	$1,500
2	31%	$103,500	$5,175	$3,571	$1,604
3	32%	$107,071	$5,354	$3,640	$1,713
4	33%	$110,711	$5,536	$3,709	$1,827
5	34%	$114,420	$5,721	$3,776	$1,945
6	35%	$118,196	$5,910	$3,841	$2,068
7	36%	$122,037	$6,102	$3,905	$2,197
8	37%	$125,942	$6,297	$3,967	$2,330
9	38%	$129,910	$6,495	$4,027	$2,468
10	39%	$133,937	$6,697	$4,085	$2,612

Section 3–6 *The Changing World of Retirement Planning*

Comparison: Taxable vs. Tax-Advantaged

By comparing a taxable investment to a tax-advantaged alternative, we can better understand the dangers of accumulating too much money in the taxable bucket over time.

Example

- An investor contributes $6,500 to each account
- Each account grows at 8%[10]
- Taxable account is taxed at 30%
    - Federal Tax: 24%
    - State Tax: 6%[11]
- Both accounts grow for 30 years[12]

Let's see what happens if we grow these two accounts side-by-side over the course of a 30 year retirement.[13]

---

[10] Assumed rates of return are not guaranteed
[11] Tax rates may vary depending on the state of residence
[12] Investors should consider current and anticipated investment horizon and income tax bracket when making a decision
[13] This example is for illustrative purposes only and is not a solicitation or recommendation of any investment strategy or product

Comparison: Taxable vs. Tax-Advantaged

■ Taxable Account   ■ Tax-Advantaged Account

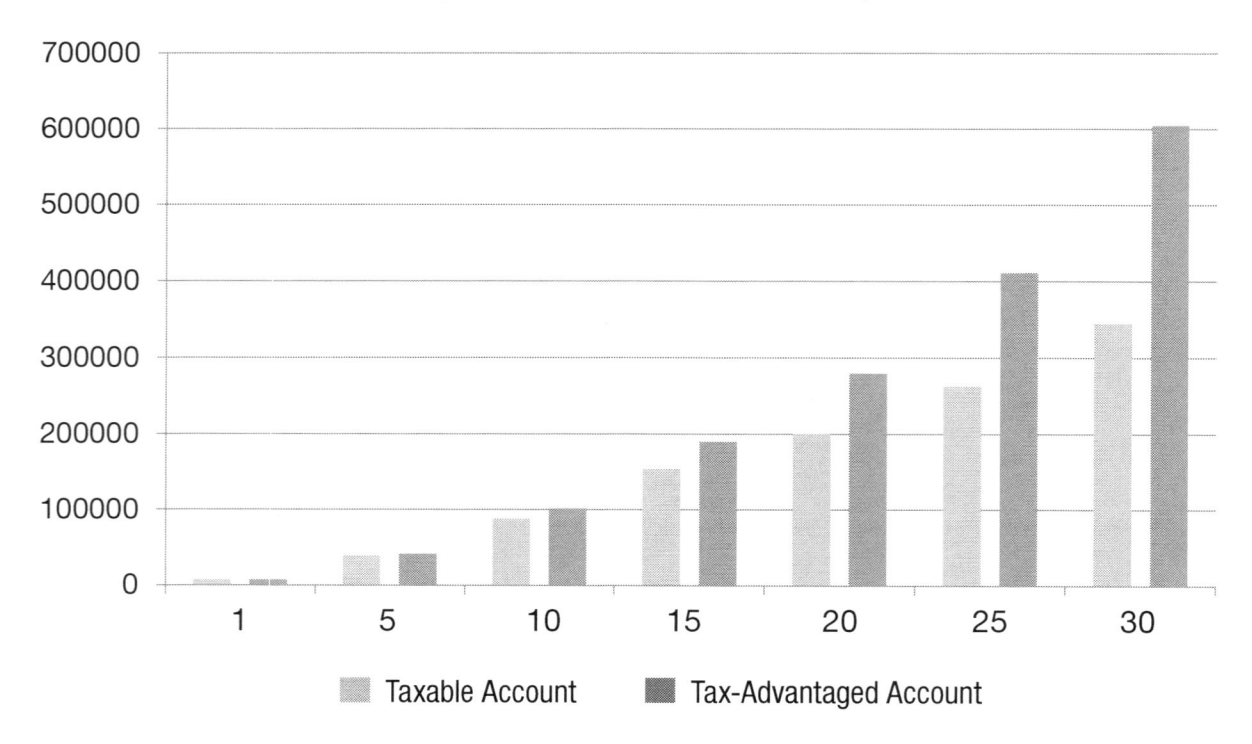

In review, because of the inherent tax-inefficiency of the taxable bucket, the ideal balance to have is about 6 months' worth of basic living expenses.

You may have more than 6 months' worth in your taxable bucket, so long as you recognize that it comes at a price. In this example, that cost was about $300,000 over a 30 year time frame.

Section 3–7   *The Changing World of Retirement Planning*

The Tax-Deferred Bucket

With the tax-deferred bucket, you don't pay taxes as your money grows. You do, however, pay taxes in retirement upon distribution. The following are examples of tax-deferred investments:

- 401(k)
- IRA
- 403(b)
- 457
- Simple IRA
- SEP

These types of plans generally have two things in common:

1. Contributions are *tax deductible*: For example, if you make $100,000 and put $10,000 into your 401(k), your taxable income reduces to $90,000.
2. Distributions are taxed as *ordinary income*: For example, when you contribute money to your 401(k), you defer the receipt of that income until distribution in retirement. At what rate are you taxed? Whatever the tax rate happens to be in the year you make the distribution.

Other Caveats

- Distributions may cause your Social Security to be taxed (more in Section 5)
- 10% penalty for distributions before age 59 ½
- Required Minimum Distributions (RMDs) begin at age 70 ½

Required Minimum Distributions

With your RMDs, the IRS forces you to take distributions at age 70 ½. Those distributions start out at 3.65% of your cumulative tax-deferred accounts and get bigger every year. The chart below shows your RMDs year by year:[14]

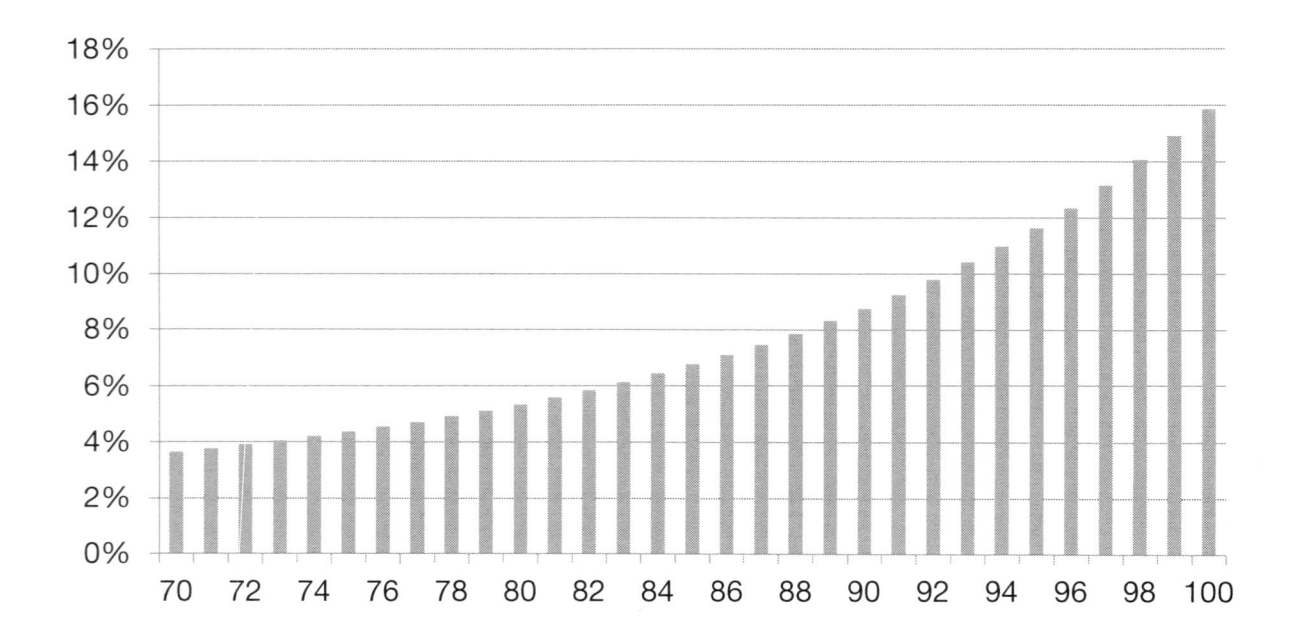

These increasing RMDs may have unintended consequences as it relates to your overall tax burden in retirement as well as affect Social Security taxation. There will be more discussion on the implications of Social Security taxation in Section 5.

[14] http://www.forbes.com/sites/baldwin/2014/03/17/rmd-tables-for-iras/

Benefits of Tax-Deferred Investing

If you believe that your tax rate in retirement is likely to be higher than it is today, then there are some good rules of thumb to follow when it comes to tax-deferred investing.

1. Contribute to your 401(k) up to the match, but not above and beyond.
2. Keep your tax-deferred balances low enough that your RMDs would be equal to or less than your standard deduction.

Rule of thumb #2 requires some explanation. Most people have very few if any deductions left by the time they retire. If that's the case the IRS does give you a deduction. It's known as the standard deduction. For a married couple that amount is as follows:

- Standard Deduction: $24,000

Example

If you were taking RMDs this year (2018), you would want your tax-deferred balances to be low enough that your RMDs would be equal to or less than your standard deduction. In that case, you would want your RMDs to be no greater than $24,000.

Given an IRA balance of $500,000 and given an initial RMD rate of 3.65%, your RMD would be $18,250. In this case your RMDs would be free from tax. This turns your tax-deferred vehicles into an ideal investment. You experienced a deduction upon contribution, your money grew tax-deferred, and you took it out without paying tax. This scenario illustrates one of the true benefits of tax-deferred investing.[15]

If, on the other hand, your tax-deferred balances were $1,000,000, your RMDs would be $36,500, much greater than your actual deductions. This would expose a portion of your RMDs to the ebb and flow of tax rates over time.

The Moral of the Story

When you have too much money in your tax-deferred bucket, you may expose yourself to higher tax rates in the future making it much more difficult to have a tax-efficient retirement.

---

[15] RMDs this high may cause Social Security taxation. See Chapter 5 for a full discussion of Provisional Income

The Tax-Advantaged Bucket

Before we get into the attributes of the tax-advantaged bucket, we must first acknowledge that there are investments that have every appearance of being tax-advantaged, but that fall short in a number of ways. Here are a few:

- Municipal Bonds
- Oil and Gas Partnerships

To qualify as tax-advantaged, an investment must embody the following attributes:

- Free from all taxes (Federal, State and Capital Gains)
- Distributions do not cause Social Security to be taxed

Examples of Tax-Advantaged Investments:

- Roth IRAs
- Roth 401(k)s
- Roth Conversions
- Some properly structured cash value life insurance policies

The Roth IRA

So long as you are at least 59 ½ when you take money out of your Roth IRA you don't pay any of the three taxes mentioned above. Second, when you take distributions from your Roth IRA, it does not count against the thresholds that cause your Social Security to be taxed.

Other attributes of the Roth IRA are as follows:

- Contribution limit: $5,500 per person
- Catch-up Provision: $6,500 per person after age 50
- Principal is liquid from day 1
- To avoid penalty on growth, you must be 59 ½ *and* have held the Roth IRA for 5 years
- To qualify for the Roth IRA, you must meet the IRS's income parameters

Income Parameters

- Married Filing Jointly: Phase out begins at $189,000 and ends at $199,000
- Single Filers: Phase out begins at $120,000 and ends at $135,000

Also, you can only contribute to a Roth IRA if you have earned income. To fully max out your Roth IRAs, you must have earned income equal to or greater than the contributions.

For example: If you were married and your adjusted gross income were $8,000, you could contribute a maximum of $8,000 to you and your spouse's cumulative Roth IRAs.

Section 3–11 *The Changing World of Retirement Planning*

If your adjusted gross income were $15,000, and you were married and over age 50, you could contribute the full $13,000 to your Roth IRAs.

The Roth 401(k):

Many companies these days have the Roth 401(k), but few advertise it. To find out if your company has one, talk to your human resources department. The Roth 401(k) is powerful because it allows you to make huge contributions to your tax-advantaged bucket on an annual basis. The contribution limits of the Roth 401(k) are:

- Contribution limit: $18,500 per year
- Catch-up Provision: $24,500 per year after age 50

Tax-Deferred or Tax-Advantaged?

So, it's probably a good time to ask the question: Should you contribute your money to tax-deferred accounts or tax-advantaged accounts? Should you pay tax on the seed or should you pay tax on the harvest? Should you do a Traditional 401(k) or a Roth 401(k)?

Now, there are all sorts of online calculators that profess to be able to tell you which one is better, but only one factor determines which account you should be doing, and it's this: Do you think your tax bracket in the future will be higher or lower than it is today?

Roth IRA vs. Traditional IRA

This diagram will help you determine whether you should invest in tax-deferred or tax-advantaged accounts for retirement. It shouldn't be any more complicated than this. Let's assume that your combined state and federal tax rate today is 30%. If that's the case then only one of three things can happen to that tax rate during your retirement. It can either go up, go down, or stay the same.

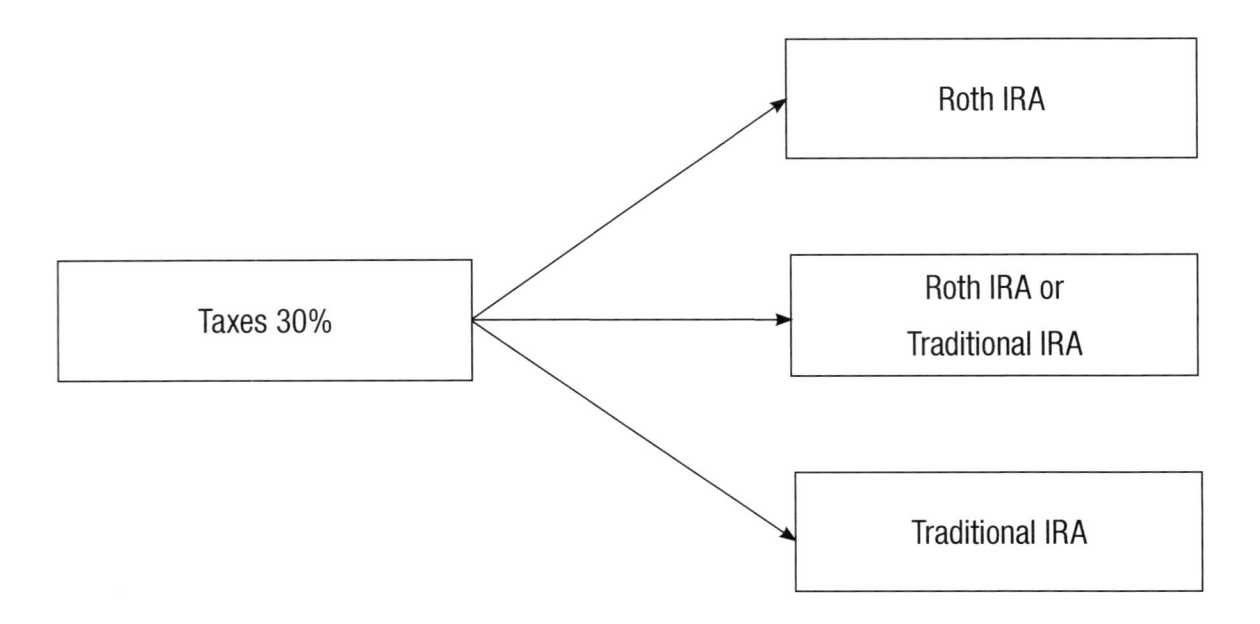

```
                          ┌─────────────┐
                       ┌─▶│   Roth IRA  │
                       │  └─────────────┘
┌─────────────┐        │  ┌─────────────┐
│  Taxes 30%  │────────┼─▶│  Roth IRA or│
└─────────────┘        │  │Traditional IRA│
                       │  └─────────────┘
                       │  ┌─────────────┐
                       └─▶│Traditional IRA│
                          └─────────────┘
```

- If your tax rate goes up, then mathematically you'll be better off doing a Roth IRA
- If your tax rate goes down, you're better off doing a Traditional IRA
- If your tax rate stays the same, it doesn't really matter which one you do, because you'll have the same after-tax cash flow in either one

The Story of Twin Brothers Doug and Gary

You may have heard the argument that Roth IRAs are deficient because you're contributing after-tax dollars. This argument suggests that since you are contributing after-tax dollars, you aren't able to contribute as much and, therefore, won't have as much money over the long-term. Let's use a little math to debunk this financial myth.

Again, the only determining factor in whether you should contribute to a Roth IRA is what you think your tax rate will be when you retire. Case closed, end of story. Let's illustrate this with the example of twin brothers Gary and Doug, both age 35.[16]

Gary is in a 30% tax bracket and likes the idea of tax deductions, so he opts for the tax-deferred approach. He decides to put $5,000 of pretax dollars in his Traditional IRA each year. He then lets those contributions grow and compound for the next 30 years. By the time he retires at age 65, he has $611,729 in his IRA. Only he doesn't really have that much because he hasn't paid taxes yet. Remember, the only dollars that really matter are those which we can spend after tax, right? Let's also assume that tax rates when Gary is 65 (suspending belief for just a moment) are still at 30%. How much of that $611,729 is left after tax, assuming that he pays tax on all distributions? The answer is $428,211.

Gary's brother Doug opts for the tax-advantaged approach with his Roth IRA. Because he's contributing dollars that have already been taxed at 30%, he can now only invest $3,500 per year. He grows these dollars over the same period of time, and then decides to retire at age 65. How much money will he have? The answer may suprise you: $428,211. It's the same as Gary, down to the last red penny.

---

[16] This example is for illustrative purposes only and is not a solicitation or recommendation of any investment strategy or product.

Traditional IRA vs. Roth IRA
Ending Balances with Same Tax Rate and Higher Future Rate

	No Change in Tax Rate		1% Increase in Tax Rate	
	Gary	Doug	Gary	Doug
Vehicle	Traditional IRA	Roth IRA	Traditional IRA	Roth IRA
Contribution Per Year	$5,000	$5,000	$5,000	$5,000
Tax Rate at Age 35	30%	30%	30%	30%
After-Tax Contribution Per Year	$5,000	$3,500	$5,000	$3,500
Average Rate of Return Per Year for 30 Years	8%	8%	8%	8%
End Value of Investment at Age 65	$611,729	$428,211	$611,729	$428,211
Tax Rate at Age 65	30%	30%	31%	31%
After-Tax End Value	$428,211	$428,211	$422,093	$428,211

Section 3–12 *The Changing World of Retirement Planning*

The Changing World of Retirement Planning Section 3–12

What's the moral of the story? If tax rates in the future are the same as they are today, it doesn't matter which IRA you choose, Roth or Traditional. However, if tax rates in the future are just one percent higher, you're better off choosing the Roth IRA. In Gary's case, 1% higher taxes means he's left with only $422,093, in which case Doug wins!

In order to figure out which type of account to invest in, you have to ask yourself what you truly believe about the future of tax rates.

The Ideal Amount in the Tax-Advantaged Bucket

If tax rates in the future are likely to be higher than they are today, there is an ideal amount to have in your tax-advantaged bucket.

- Everything above and beyond the ideal amounts in the taxable bucket (more than 6 months) should be shifted to tax-advantaged
- Everything above and beyond the ideal amounts in the tax-deferred bucket (RMDs equal to or less than your standard deduction) should be shifted to tax-advantaged[17]

Remember, that's only if you think that tax rates in the future will be higher than they are today. So, again, you really have to ask yourself where you think tax rates will be in the year you take these dollars out.

---

[17] To avoid Social Security taxation, balances in the tax-deferred bucket may need to be further reduced to stay below Provisional Income thresholds. See Chapter 5 for a full discussion of Provisional Income

In Summary

If taxes in the future are likely to be higher than they are today, then we have to be very thoughtful about where we choose to grow and compound our retirement savings. As we prepare for a retirement with an eye towards tax efficiency, we must keep in mind the following:

- There are three basic types of accounts in which to save for retirement: taxable, tax-deferred and tax-advantaged
- If taxes are likely to be higher in the future, there is a mathematically ideal amount to have in each account or "bucket"
- The Taxable Bucket should have 6 months' worth of basic income needs
- The Tax-Deferred Bucket should have a low enough balance that RMDs can be offset by your standard deduction
- The Tax-Advantaged bucket should hold anything above and beyond the ideal amounts in the taxable and tax-deferred buckets
- A true Tax-Advantaged investment is free from all 3 types of tax and does not contribute to the thresholds that cause Social Security taxation

SECTION FOUR

Maximizing Social Security

Introduction

If you have too much money in either of your first two buckets (taxable and tax-deferred) it may cause your Social Security to be taxed. When your Social Security gets taxed, it forces you to spend down your other assets to compensate.

In this section we will cover the following:

- The causes of Social Security taxation
- The definition of Provisional Income
- The Social Security thresholds you need to be aware of
- The real cost of Social Security taxation
- Strategies to reduce or eliminate Social Security taxation[18]

---

[18] This section presents a general overview of certain rules related to Social Security and the ideas presented are not individualized for your particular situation. This information is based on current law which can be changed at any time.

The Changing World of Retirement Planning   Section 4–1

What is Provisional Income?

To understand why our Social Security gets taxed, it's important to understand "Provisional Income".

Definition: The income the IRS tracks to determine if your Social Security will be taxed.

What Counts as Provisional Income?

1. All earned income
2. Distributions from Qualified Plans (IRAs, 401(k)s, etc.)
3. Required Minimum Distributions (RMDs)
4. 1099s from taxable bucket
5. Pensions
6. Rental income
7. Interest from Municipal Bonds
8. One-half of your Social Security

The IRS adds up all your Provisional Income and, based on that total, and your marital status, determines what percentage of your Social Security benefits will become taxed. That percentage of your Social Security is then taxed at your highest marginal tax rate.

The Changing World of Retirement Planning   *Section 4-2*

Provisional Income Thresholds (Married Filers)

The Provisional Income threshold for married couples are as follows:

Provisional Income	Percent of Social Security Subject to Tax
Under $32,000	0%
$32,000 to $44,000	Up to 50%
Over $44,000	Up to 85%

Provisional Income Thresholds (Single Filers)

The Provisional Income threshold for Single Filers are as follows:

Provisional Income	Percent of Social Security Subject to Tax
Under $25,000	0%
$25,000 to $34,000	Up to 50%
Over $34,000	Up to 85%

Example of Social Security Taxation

Bob and Mary's Provisional Income is as follows:

- Pension: $70,000 per year
- Required Minimum Distributions: $30,000 per year
- ½ of Social Security: $15,000 per year

Total Provisional Income: $115,000

Because of Bob and Mary's Provisional Income, 85% of their Social Security becomes taxable at their highest marginal tax bracket.

Assuming a 22% federal tax rate (by the way, most states do not charge state tax for Social Security), and assuming a Social Security benefit of $30,000, then 85% of that amount would be subject to taxation. 85% of $30,000 is $25,500. When we multiply $25,500 by 22%, we find that Bob and Mary's total Social Security tax bill is $5,610 per year!

Social Security Taxation

Because of Social Security taxation, Bob and Mary experienced the following:

- Lost $5,610 in yearly Social Security benefits
- To compensate, they would likely take distributions from their IRA
- At 28% tax rates (22% federal, 6% state), they would need to withdraw $7,792 to net $5,610
- Total cost of Social Security Taxation = $7,792 per year!

The Long-Term Costs of Social Security Taxation

The damage doesn't stop here, however. Bob and Mary do lose $7,792 because of Social Security taxation, but they also lose the opportunity cost that goes along with it. What is opportunity cost?

Definition: The cost of an alternative that must be forgone in order to pursue a certain action. Put another way, the benefits you could have received by taking an alternative action.[19]

In other words, when you give up that $7,792, not only do you give up that amount, but you give up what it could have earned for you had you been able to keep it and invest it over the balance of your retirement. If Bob and Mary had been able to keep that $7,792 every year and invest it at 8% over the next 20 years, how much better off could they be? $385,103 better off! So, the total cost of Social Security taxation can take a huge toll on one's retirement over time.

[19] Investopedia.com

Social Security Reality Check

In reality, Social Security taxation is much worse than what's been described. How so? Because Social Security rises to keep up with inflation every year. So, you may pay $5,610 in Social Security taxation this year, but next year your Social Security check will be even bigger. The bigger the check, the bigger the tax bill. The bigger the tax bill, the bigger the distribution from your IRA or 401(k) to compensate.

Avoiding Social Security Taxation

Given the realities of Provisional Income, is there any possible way to avoid Social Security taxation? The key is to keep your Provisional Income below the thresholds of which we spoke earlier. This can be done by repositioning a portion of your assets to the tax-advantaged bucket, such that your remaining streams of income keep you below these thresholds. By accumulating the right amounts of money in the right types of accounts, you can reduce Provisional Income to acceptable levels and keep your Social Security free from tax!

Ensure that Your Provisional Income Stays Below Thresholds

Distributions from true tax-advantaged investments do not count as Provisional Income.

What investment accounts qualify as tax-advantaged?

1. Roth IRAs
2. Roth 401(k)s
3. Roth Conversions
4. Some forms of Cash Value Life Insurance

Q: What is the single greatest contributor to Social Security taxation?

A: Having too much money in your:

1. IRAs
2. 401(k)s
3. Pensions, etc.

Reposition tax-deferred assets to tax-advantaged accounts to reduce Provisional Income and avoid Social Security taxation.

Pensions and Social Security Taxation

So, how does all this change if you have a large pension? Remember, 100% of your pension income is counted as Provisional Income. So, if your pension is large enough, it can almost guarantee that your Social Security will be taxable. So, while it's nice to have that guaranteed income in retirement, that income comes at a price.

So, is there any way to get around this? Before making your pension election, explore whether your company offers a lump sum distribution option. This would allow you to roll the lump sum value of your pension into an IRA. And, once it's in an IRA, you could then convert it to a Roth IRA, eliminating it as a source of Provisional Income forever. This may dramatically increase the likelihood that you could get your Social Security free from tax.

In Summary

To this point we have suggested that if tax rates in the future are higher than they are today, then there is a mathematically ideal amount to have in each of the three retirement buckets:

- Taxable Bucket: 6 months' worth of living expenses
- Tax-Deferred Bucket: Balance should be low enough that RMDs at 70 ½ are equal to or less than your standard deduction[20]
- Tax-Advantaged Bucket: Everything above and beyond the ideal balances in the taxable and tax-deferred bucket should be repositioned to tax-advantaged

In this section we also discussed the mechanics of Social Security taxation as well as the impact it may have on your cash flow in retirement. To insulate yourself from the impact of Social Security taxation, you must ensure that your Provisional Income levels stay below the thresholds required by the IRS. This is most easily accomplished by ensuring that you have accumulated the ideal balances in each of the three retirement buckets.

---

[20] When calculating the ideal balance in the tax-deferred bucket, keep in mind that one-half of Social Security counts as Provisional Income. Therefore, these balances may need to be adjusted to stay below minimum Provisional Income thresholds

SECTION FIVE

Long-Term Care Planning

Introduction

An untimely long-term care event during retirement may unravel many of the benefits brought about by the strategies we've discussed to this point.

In this section, we will discuss:

- The effect long-term care may have on your retirement
- Medicaid spend-down rules
- "Community Spouse" rules
- Four common alternatives to pay for long-term care
- Recent innovations in long-term care planning

The Old Paradigm

Let's begin by discussing the "Old Paradigm" when it comes to planning for a long-term care event:

- Medicare will pay for long-term care expenses
- Assets can be gifted away in order to qualify for Medicaid faster
- Children can take care of aging parents
- "I won't end up needing long-term care."
- There are only three ways to mitigate long-term care risks:
    - Self-insure
    - Rely on family members
    - Buy expensive long-term care insurance

The New Paradigm

The latest statistics go a long way towards debunking the traditional paradigms when it comes to long-term care:

- National average cost of long-term care is $6,753 to $7,543 per month
- 70% of retirees will need long-term care at some time in their retirement
- Medicare does not pay for long-term care
- Medicaid only steps in when you're broke!
- The Medicaid look-back period is now 60 months
- Long-term care can destroy a lifetime of savings before it reaches the next generation
- Children are often incapable or resentful of taking on long-term care duties
- Expensive long-term care insurance is no longer the only way to safeguard against a long-term care event[21]

Confronting the realities of long-term care requires a perspective that accounts for new legislative and statistical realities that are unique to the 21st century.

---

[21] http://www.longtermcarelink.net/eldercare/medicaid_long_term_care.htm

Medicaid Spend-down Rules

Before we discuss the role Medicaid may play in your efforts to pay for the cost of long-term care, it's important to understand how Medicaid is defined:

- **Definition**: A joint federal and state program that helps low-income individuals or families pay for the costs associated with long-term medical and custodial care, provided they qualify. Although largely funded by the federal government, Medicaid is run by the state where coverage may vary.

So, in essence, Medicaid is only available to people who meet certain qualifications, i.e., you can't afford to pay for the cost of long-term care on your own.

Asset Qualifications

- A nursing home patient is not allowed to have more than $2,400 worth of "countable assets"
- The "community spouse" living at home is allowed to keep a limited amount of "countable assets" to live on:
    - $120,900 of liquid assets
    - one house
    - one car

Income Qualifications

- Community spouse is allowed to keep a Minimum Monthly Maintenance Needs Allowance (MMMNA)
- MMMNA varies by state, but averages around $2,500 per month

For these reasons experts cite long-term care as one of the greatest threats to your retirement. Many couples save their entire lives only to see their entire estate decimated in the waning years of their life through long-term care spend-down.

How Will You Pay for Long-Term Care Expenses?

So, we recognize that LTC is a huge risk that needs to be mitigated, but how does one go about doing it? There are 4 common ways to pay for long-term care:

- Plan to pay the costs yourself
- Ask your family members to take care of you
- Purchase a traditional long-term care insurance policy
- Purchase a life insurance policy with long-term care features

Which one of these options is right for you? It depends largely upon your situation and your individual needs.

Traditional Long-Term Care Insurance

Let's begin by evaluating traditional long-term care insurance. The following are a few considerations when evaluating this option:

- Underwriting is based on morbidity, not mortality
  - Morbidity is the likelihood you will have a long-term care event
  - Mortality is the likelihood you will die
- Joint or back issues may disqualify applicants

- Insured must no longer be able to perform 2 of 6 activities of daily living
    - Eating
    - Bathing
    - Dressing
    - Toileting
    - Transferring (walking)
    - Continence
- Premiums are not guaranteed and may rise
- Coverage is typically use-it-or-lose-it
- Expenses paid through reimbursement
    - Insured pays for coverage out of own pocket
    - Submits receipts to long-term care insurance company
    - Certain expenses may be excluded from reimbursement

Even though there are a lot of perceived negatives when it comes to traditional long-term care insurance, many couples choose to utilize it given the peace of mind it affords them.

An Alternate Approach: Life Insurance

Some insurance companies offer life insurance policies that have chronic illness benefits that have the same triggers as traditional long-term care insurance. While these policies cover the same types of conditions, the policies themselves have a number of material differences. These include the following:

- Underwriting is based on mortality (life expectancy), not morbidity
- Joint and back problems don't generally figure into the underwriting process
- Premiums may be guaranteed never to rise
- If the insured dies never having needed long-term care, the death benefit can be passed onto heirs
- Benefits are paid based on indemnity (no receipts required), not reimbursement
- Death benefit is given to insured in advance of death, typically 25% at a time over 4 years. This benefit may be discounted at the time of disbursement depending on the age of the insured.

Here's an example of how a life insurance death benefit might be used to pay for long-term care expenses:[22]

- The insured has a $400,000 death benefit
- The insured can no longer perform 2 of 6 activities of daily living
- A doctor writes a letter stating as much
- The insurance company advances 25% of the $400,000 death benefit ($100,000) every year for 4 years (no receipts required).
- The $100,000 annual benefit may be subject to discounting depending on the age of the insured when the chronic illness arises

In short, life insurance is not always the best option when looking to mitigate the cost of long-term care but it can be an alternative that provides flexibility and security that contrasts with some of the more traditional approaches.

[22] The hypothetical example is for illustrative purposes only. Each individual's situation or policy is different.

In Summary

Long-term care planning is a critical part of preparing for retirement in the 21st century. A lifetime of savings can be "spent down" in the waning years of one's retirement to pay for the ever-increasing costs of care. The following should be considered in determining how to best mitigate the risk of long-term care:

- A long-term care event may have a devastating impact on your retirement
- Medicaid steps in only after "spend-down"
- The community spouse retains a Minimum Monthly Maintenance Needs Allowance (MMMNA) of around $2,500, one house, one car and up to $120,900 of liquid assets
- There are 4 ways to handle long-term care expenses
  - Self-insure
  - Rely on family
  - Purchase long-term care insurance
  - Use life insurance that doubles as long-term care insurance